THE LITTLE BOOK OF

PRAYERS

For Jessica

*The publishers would like to thank
the Revd. Maria Schleger for her help
in making this selection.*

KINGFISHER BOOKS
Grisewood & Dempsey Inc.
95 Madison Avenue
New York, New York 10016

This edition published in 1994
First published in the United States in hardcover in 1993
2 4 6 8 10 9 7 5 3 1

Library of Congress Cataloging-in-Publication Data
The Little book of prayers / compiled by Caroline Walsh: illustrated
by Inga Moore. — 1st American ed.
p. cm.
Includes index.
Summary: A collection of familiar and less well-known prayers
1. Prayers. [1. Prayer books and devotions.]   I. Walsh,
Caroline.   II. Moore, Inga, ill.   III. Title: Prayers.
BL560.L585   1993
291.4'3–dc20   92-30860   CIP   AC

ISBN 1-85697-523-1

Printed in Hong Kong

THE LITTLE BOOK OF

PRAYERS

Selected by Caroline Walsh • Illustrated by Inga Moore

Kingfisher Books

Contents

Contents

Now another day is breaking,
Sleep was sweet but so is waking.
Dear Lord, I promised you last night
Never again to sulk or fight.
Such vows are easier to keep
When a child is sound asleep.
Today, O Lord, for your dear sake,
I'll try to keep them when awake.

OGDEN NASH

Dear Father, bless this day,
And bless me too;
Bless me in all I say,
And all I do.

ELFRIDA VIPONT

Dear Father,
      Hear and bless
Your beasts
      And singing birds:
And guard
      With tenderness
Small things
      That have no words.

ANON

The year's at the spring,
And the day's at the morn;
Morning's at seven
The hill-side's dew-pearl'd;
The lark's on the wing;
The snail's on the thorn;
God's in his heaven —
All's right with the world!

ROBERT BROWNING

Lord, thou knowest how busy I must be this day.
If I forget thee, do not thou forget me.

SIR JACOB ASTLEY

For all that has been — Thanks!
To all that shall be — Yes!

DAG HAMMARSKJÖLD

God be in my head,
And in my understanding;

God be in my eyes,
And in my looking;

God be in my mouth,
And in my speaking;

God be in my heart,
And in my thinking;

God be at my end,
And at my departing.

from the Sarum Primer

God grant me the serenity
to accept the things I cannot change,
the courage to change the things I can,
and the wisdom to know the difference.

REINHOLD NIEBUHR

All through this day, Lord,
Let me touch the lives of others for good
By the power of your quickening Spirit,
Whether through the word I speak,
The prayer I breathe, or the life I live,
In the name of Jesus Christ.

MARY SUMNER

Oh God, make the door of this house wide enough
to receive all who need human love and fellowship;
narrow enough to shut out all envy, pride, and strife.

BISHOP THOMAS KEN

We are going home to many who cannot read.
So, Lord, make us to be Bibles
so that those who cannot read the Bible can read it in us.

Prayer from China

We can do no great things,
Only small things with great love.

MOTHER TERESA OF CALCUTTA

O you gotta get a glory
        In the work you do,
A Halleluiah chorus
        In the heart of you.
Paint or tell a story,
        Sing or shovel coal,
But you gotta get a glory
        Or the job lacks soul.

from a spiritual

Go tell it on the mountain,
    Over the hills and everywhere.
Go tell it on the mountain
    That Jesus Christ is born.

from a spiritual

Breton Fisherman's Prayer

Dear God, be good to me;
The sea is so wide,
And my boat is so small.

O heavenly Father, protect and bless
all things that have breath:
Guard them from all evil
and let them sleep in peace.

ALBERT SCHWEITZER

Be thou a bright flame before me,
Be thou a guiding star above me,
Be thou a smooth path below me,
Be thou a kindly shepherd behind me,
Today — tonight — and forever.

ST. COLUMBA OF IONA

Gaelic Blessing

May the road rise to meet you.
May the wind be always at your back.
May the sun shine warm upon your face.
May the rains fall softly upon your fields
    until we meet again.
May God hold you in the hollow of his hand.

Gaelic Prayer

As the rain hides the stars,
as the autumn mist hides the hills,
as the clouds veil the blue of the sky,
so the dark happenings of my lot
hide the shining of your face from me.
Yet, if I may hold your hand in the darkness,
it is enough.
Since I know that, though I may stumble in my going,
You do not fall.

I believe in the sun even when it does not shine
I believe in love even when I do not feel it
I believe in God even when He is silent.

Inscription on the walls of a cellar in Cologne, Germany,
where Jews hid from the Nazis.

When I despise myself or the world
let me find your image within me again.
Blessed are you O Lord,
who have made me as you wanted me.

ANON

O God,
I try and think about you
but I can't see your face.
I try and talk to you,
but you don't answer me.
How can I know you love me
unless I feel your touch?
And how can I reach out to you
if you have gone away?
I want to understand you,
but you are too hard for me;
so I am waiting here in the dark,
waiting for you, O God.

JANET MORLEY

Praise God, from whom all blessings flow;
Praise him, all creatures here below;
Praise him above, you heavenly host;
Praise Father, Son, and Holy Ghost.

BISHOP THOMAS KEN

For every cup and plateful
God make us truly grateful.

Traditional Grace

The 23rd Psalm

The Lord is my shepherd, I shall not want; he makes
me lie down in green pastures. He leads me beside
still waters; he restores my soul. He leads me in paths
of righteousness for his name's sake. Even though
I walk through the valley of the shadow of death,
I fear no evil; for thou art with me; thy rod and
thy staff, they comfort me. Thou preparest a table
before me in the presence of my enemies;

thou anointest my head with oil, my cup overflows.
Surely goodness and mercy shall follow me all the
days of my life; and I shall dwell in the house of the
Lord for ever.

Lamb of God, I look to thee,
Thou shalt my example be;
Thou art gentle, meek, and mild,
Thou wast once a little child.

CHARLES WESLEY

God bless all those that I love;
God bless all those that love me:
God bless all those that love those that I love
And all those that love those that love me.

from a New England Sampler

Thank you for the world so sweet,
Thank you for the food we eat.
Thank you for the birds that sing,
Thank you, God, for everything.

E. RUTTER LEATHAM

The Breastplate of St. Patrick

I bind unto myself today
  The power of God to hold and lead,
His eye to watch, his might to stay,
  His ear to hearken to my need.
The wisdom of my God to teach,
  His hand to guide, his shield to ward;
The word of God to give me speech,
  His heavenly host to be my guard.

Christ be with me, Christ within me,
Christ behind me, Christ before me,
Christ beside me, Christ to win me,
Christ beneath me, Christ above me,
Christ in quiet, Christ in danger,
Christ in mouth of friend or stranger.

Praised be my Lord by our brother the wind;
and by air and cloud, calms and all weather,
by which you uphold life in all creatures.

ST. FRANCIS OF ASSISI

He prayeth best,
Who loveth best
All things both
Great and small;
For the dear God
Who loveth us,
He made and loveth all.

SAMUEL TAYLOR COLERIDGE

Watch, Lord,
with those who wake,
or watch, or weep tonight,
and give your angels
charge over those who sleep.
Tend your sick ones,
O Lord Jesus Christ,
rest your weary ones;
bless your dying ones;
soothe your suffering ones;
pity your afflicted ones;
shield your joyous ones.
And all for your love's sake.

ST. AUGUSTINE

All praise to thee, my God, this night,
For all the blessings of the light;
Keep me, O keep me, King of Kings,
Beneath thy own almighty wings.

BISHOP THOMAS KEN

Lighten our darkness, we beseech thee, O Lord;
and by thy great mercy defend us from all perils
and dangers of this night; for the love of thine
only Son, our Savior Jesus Christ. Amen.

from THE BOOK OF COMMON PRAYER

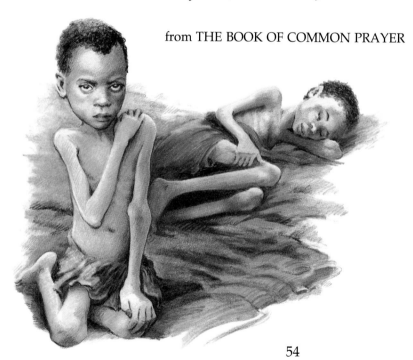

The Lord's Prayer

Our Father, who art in heaven,
Hallowed be thy name.
Thy kingdom come,
Thy will be done,
On earth as it is in heaven.
Give us this day our daily bread;
And forgive us our trespasses
As we forgive those
   who trespass against us;
And lead us not into temptation,
But deliver us from evil.
For thine is the kingdom, the power,
And the glory
Now and for ever. Amen.

Loving Jesus, gentle Lamb,
In thy gracious hands I am;
Make me, Savior, what thou art,
Live thyself within my heart.

CHARLES WESLEY

Preserve us, O Lord, while waking,
and guard us while sleeping;
that awake we may watch with Christ,
and asleep we may rest in peace.

Evening Prayer

Now I lay me down to sleep,
I pray thee, Lord, thy child to keep;
Thy love to guard me through the night
And wake me in the morning light.

Night Prayer

Dear Jesus, as a hen covers her chicks with her wings
to keep them safe, do thou this dark night protect us
under your golden wings.

Prayer from India

I believe that God is in me as the sun is in
the color and fragrance of a flower — the
light in my darkness, the Voice in my silence.

HELEN KELLER

Acknowledgments

For permission to reproduce copyright material, acknowledgment and thanks are due to the following:

Curtis Brown Ltd. and Andre Deutsch Ltd for "Now Another Day is Breaking" by Ogden Nash from *I Wouldn't Have Missed It*. Copyright © 1961, 1962 Ogden Nash; Alfred A. Knopf, Inc. for "For all that has been — Thanks!" by Dag Hammarskjöld from *Markings* translated by W.H. Auden and Leif Sjoberg, translation copyright © 1964 by Alfred A. Knopf, Inc. and Faber & Faber, Ltd.; The Mothers' Union for "All through this day, Lord" by Mary Sumner, founder of the Mothers' Union; Victor Gollancz Ltd. for a short prayer by Albert Schweitzer from *God of a Hundred Names* compiled by Barbara Greene and Victor Gollancz; Janet Morley for "O God, I try and think about you".

Every effort has been made to obtain permission from copyright holders. If, regrettably, any omissions have been made, we shall be pleased to make suitable corrections in any reprint.